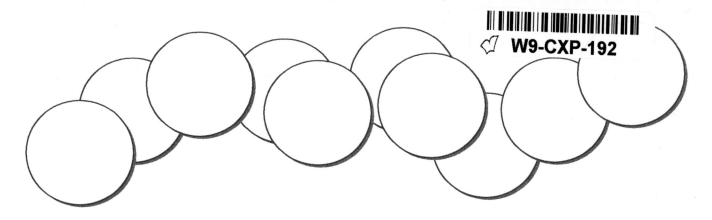

Making Literature Circles Come Alive

A Time-Saving Resource by Amy Humphreys

Pieces of Learning

CLC0289
© 2003 Pieces of Learning
Marion IL
ISBN 978-1-931334-22-8
www.piecesoflearning.com
Cover by John Steele

Table of Contents

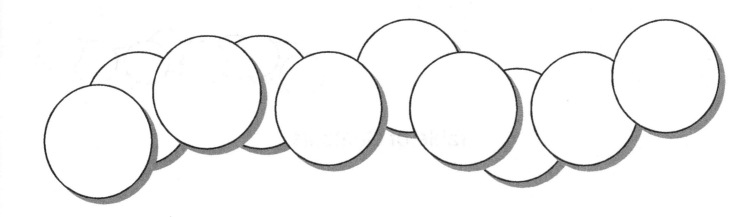

Amy Hamra works with students in grades 4-8 as a facilitator of gifted services for a mid-sized district in central Illinois. In November 2000, she received National Board certification in Early Adolescent English Language Arts. Amy presents numerous workshops related to drama, writing, and higher level thinking each year.

Prior to becoming an educator, Amy worked as a writer for two advertising agencies, produced radio interview clips for use by the wire services and even delivered singing telegrams. She has a BA in communications from Western Illinois University, an Ed.M. and 40+ hours of post graduate study in education from the University of Illinois. Amy and her daughter spend their free time reading and enjoying the great outdoors.

Making Literature Circles Come Alive

Introduction - I tried a variety of approaches to literature circles over a 10 year span with little success. While the idea of having students work in small discussion groups was attractive, the reality was lackluster at best. I'd try them for awhile only to find myself abandoning that instructional framework when I witnessed the lame discussions that were taking place even among my best learners.

Before throwing in the towel for the final time I decided to precisely analyze what was going wrong. I was a competent teacher but I was obviously missing some key tactic that would be "the answer". Thoughtful analysis paid off. I soon learned it didn't matter what cute names were used for the various roles or how we scheduled the discussions and reading sessions. My investigation identified two key weaknesses in our literature circles that had to be remedied:

1. **Quality Questions** - My students were using nearly 100% low-level questions that made their conversations more like quiz bowls rather than true explorations of the book. I used high-level questions with them in class but had never shown them how they were created. If you're asking students to run effective discussions you must teach them about various levels of questions.

❑ Job one: spend several class sessions and directly teach students how to craft top-quality discussion questions.

2. **Engaging Sharing Tools** - Students had assigned lit circle roles. Now they even came with lists of high-level questions to discuss. Better... but boring! They needed other ways to carry out their responsibilities to keep interest and engagement high.

❑ Job two: provide students with quality examples of sharing tools appropriate for the various roles. These tools and activities have to elicit high-level thinking and get all group members actively exploring the characters, conflicts, setting, vocabulary, author's craft and real-world connections related to the novel.

So, take a two-week break from regular reading instruction and lay a solid foundation for your students using the powerful and effective activities in this book. The payoffs are well worth the investment and will result in dynamic, engaged, student-led literature circles that get quality results.

5

Setting the Stage for Lit Circles

- Students learn to recognize, develop and classify high-level questions using Bloom's Taxonomy

- Students craft questions using their favorite picture books

- Whole class, small group & individual activities help students apply questioning to lit circle discussions

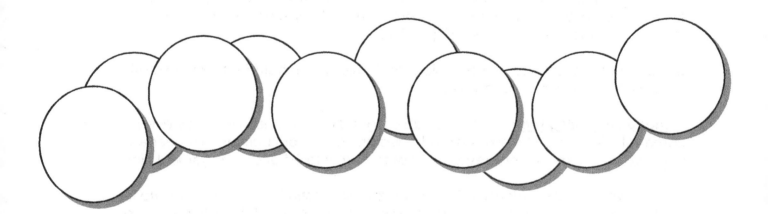

6

Setting the Stage

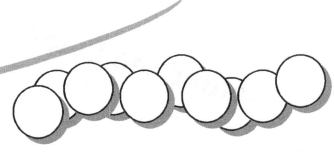

Q: Why is Setting the Stage essential training?
A: Because quality thinking doesn't just happen.
Although the idea of literature circles sounds attractive, there are numerous pitfalls that can seriously undermine the approach. Simply having students work in such groups does not guarantee quality thinking and active discussions take place. In fact, it doesn't matter how the groups are formed, what the jobs are called, or what books are selected. Discussions won't have the power and depth necessary to fully explore quality literature unless your students have a thorough understanding of high-level thinking and questioning. Students must be shown how to develop questions with several possible responses that require solid reasoning and original thinking. (This book provides that vital foundation.) Quality literature should promote critical and creative thinking. **Setting the Stage** shows students and teachers how to craft discussion questions to achieve that goal.

Q: How does Setting the Stage work?
A: Simply and powerfully!
Setting the Stage is designed to be completed in five to eight sessions. It includes a powerful combination of whole class, small group, and individual activities that teach students how to recognize and produce top-level thinking. The activities are engaging, effective, and ready-to-go. Just read the step-by-step plans, make the necessary copies, and get ready for some awesome discussions. Use the extra activity sheets for periodic review or for individual assessment.

Q: What should I focus on?
A: Discussion and modeling.
Frequently we want all students to reach consensus on a particular answer. That isn't necessarily true in **Setting the Stage**. In fact, disagreements about how to classify a particular task or question stimulate exactly the kind of high-level thinking we want students to use. The important thing is for learners to explain and support the reasoning they used to reach their decisions. So when things get lively, remember that spirited debates promote quality thinking and engaged learning!

Q: What happens afterwards?
A: Transfer these skills to lit circles.
Once you've completed **Setting the Stage**, students will be prepared to enter lit circle discussions with a totally new level of competence. Should you want specific ideas for exploring novels using drama, games, visual tools and various discussion activities, proceed to **Dynamic Sharing Tools**. In addition to detailed guidelines for structuring effective lit circles, it includes instructions for creating 12 sharing tools that are all-time student favorites. They're an ideal way for students to apply their new understanding of high-level thinking and questioning in lit circles. The activities also serve as springboards for new sharing tools your students will want to create once they have had some initial successes.

7

Setting the Stage

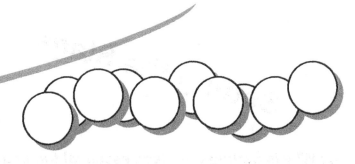

Part 1
- Have students respond to question one on the **Personal Reflections** form. It is a simple pre-assessment about thinking. Let them know it is fine to say they know nothing about various levels of thinking. Most students don't have any experience with the topic. Students should sign and date their work. Collect the forms and place them in a file folder. The final two questions will be completed by students at the end of the unit.
- Discuss low, medium, and high levels of thinking and the words that signal each. If desired, allow students to work in teams to create a rhythmic chant with motions to help memorize the three posters. Copy and laminate the low, medium, and high mini-posters on pages 18-20 and hang them in a spot where you can refer to them during activities and class discussions. Provide each student a copy of page 17 as an individual reference sheet to use when developing quality discussion questions and activities.
- Move students into groups of 3 or 4. Pass out **task cards**. They should place each task under the **low, medium, or high slips**. Share and discuss their decisions full-class. Make sure students tie their LMH placements to the ideas contained in the chants.
- If time allows, read a fun picture book. Pose questions for students. Rather than answering the question, have students decide if they represent a low, medium or high level of thinking. Sample questions and tasks for Mike Thaler's ***The Librarian from the Black Lagoon*** have been provided as an example.

Part 2
- Once again place students in small groups and pass out the **Mountain Bike** activity. Have teams decide at which level each task would be found. Students can raise **low, medium, and high slips** to indicate their answers. Discuss their decisions full-class. You will soon find some students wanting to combine the cards such as medium-low. That need for greater precision and the lack of consensus between groups is a wonderful opportunity to extend and clarify thinking. It also paves the way for a more precise system to describe thinking. Introduce the **Levels of Thinking Pyramid** to those students needing the extension. Focus on the six key terms in Bloom's Taxonomy and the verbs associated with each. Provide each student with a laminated copy to keep in a folder. For those not ready for the precision of Bloom's, provide them with a pyramid, but continue having the students use low, medium and high designations. Some may never move beyond LMH all year and that is fine.
- Revisit the **Mountain Bike** activity using the **Six Levels** strips and the **Pyramid**.
- If time allows, read another picture book. Using the **Bloom's** or **LMH slips**, have students decide at what level various questions or tasks fall. Discuss their choices and reasoning. Again, focus on the verbs associated with each level. Tasks and questions for ***More than Anything Else*** by Marie Bradby have been provided as a second example.

8

Copyright 2003 Pieces of Learning

Setting the Stage

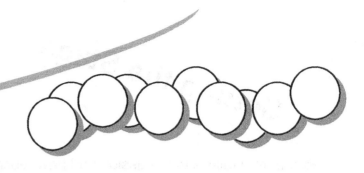

Part 3

- Give students the **Sand Volleyball** activity and rank the tasks in order from lowest to highest. It is best to begin by having them decide if a task is at the low, medium or high level. Then they can move to Bloom's. Referring to the Pyramid sheets is essential. For students requiring instructional modifications, you may continue with basic LMH distinctions. Discuss their choices and reasoning. Make sure to focus on the verbs associated with each level.
- Pass out the **Literature Tasks**. Working in pairs, have students analyze the level of thinking required by each task or question. Together they should discuss how questions or tasks falling below the application level can be rewritten. (Often just adding the word "why" can turn a basic knowledge or comprehension level question into something far more sophisticated.) Share their ideas in a full-class setting so students learn from the ideas presented by classmates.

Part 4

- Have students work independently using the **In-line Skating** sheet and share the results through class discussion.
- Read another picture book. This time have students work in pairs and develop a set of tasks and questions related to the story using the **On Your Own** sheet. On a separate sheet of paper have learners specify which Bloom's word best describes the level of the questions they created. Have students exchange papers and determine the level of each item. Discuss the results full-class and explore controversial tasks and questions. Those students needing additional teacher support can complete this task in a small group with your direction.
- Next, discuss how students can use their new understanding of thinking as they develop quality discussion questions and activities for novels they are reading.

Part 5

- Have students complete **Take Me to Your Leader** in pairs. This wacky, but highly effective activity is from the book ***But I Only Have 45 Minutes!*** available from Pieces of Learning. In the simulation, students serve as members of an advisory council on the planet Zoargut. Together, they are responsible for evaluating six candidates applying for the position of Chief of Exploration. These aliens have been sent to Earth to investigate an immensely popular substance called candy. Students will analyze the quality of thinking exhibited in each alien's report using Bloom's Taxonomy. Two activities included in ***Setting the Stage***, **Cinderella** and **Jets**, can be used as well as **Take Me to Your Leader**.

Part 6

- Using a current science or social studies lesson, have students rate the end-of-section questions using Bloom's. Share and discuss their classifications.
- Working in teams, have them create one low, one medium and one high-level activity or question related to the content. Have students underline the key verb in each of their questions.

9

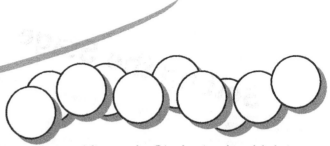

Return to a full-class discussion and have each team present its work. Students should determine where the items fall in Bloom's Taxonomy. After that, the members of the team can share their thoughts about the level of thinking reflected in various questions. If those sharing simply stand up and tell about the items and the levels, it doesn't allow for thoughtful analysis by the rest of the class. This concept must be well understood before students begin developing sharing tools for use in literature circles.

- Using a non-fiction picture book, continue practicing the technique of developing questions or activities at the various levels. Ample modeling of this process is essential for student mastery.
- Students should complete the remaining two questions on the **Personal Reflections** form. They should sign, date, and place it in their portfolio.

Remember...

Knowledge and comprehension questions generally have one right answer. That doesn't leave much to discuss. When applying their skills students should strive to develop questions or tasks that can have several possible responses and require solid reasoning, original thinking, or judgments with solid supporting arguments based on information from the novel. This means operating at the application level or above in Bloom's Taxonomy. Complete guidelines on helping students apply their new understanding of quality thinking and questioning in lit circles can be found in *Dynamic Sharing Tools*.

Picture Books

The following picture books work well when introducing various levels of thinking to students in grades 4-12. Older students thoroughly enjoy using them, especially if you begin with something humorous such as those indicated with an asterisk. Feel free to substitute other titles from your library, because any book that generates conversation works well. Although "serious" books allow you to develop more substantial discussion questions and tasks, mixing them with humorous books makes the process very engaging for students, yet still helps students refine their abilities to identify and eventually craft questions and tasks at various levels.

The Librarian from the Black Lagoon by Mike Thaler*
Miss Nelson is Missing! by James Marshall
A Bad Case of Stripes by David Shannon
Follow the Drinking Gourd by Jeanette Winter
Cinder Edna by Ellen Jackson*
Bubba the Cowboy Prince, a Fractured Texas Tale by Helen Ketterman*
Dear Willy Rudd by Libba Gray
Dog Breath by Dav Pilkey*
The Fourth Little Pig from Steck-Vaughn Publishers*
More than Anything Else by Marie Bradby
Tacky the Penguin by Helen Lester*
The Other Side by Jacqueline Woodson

10

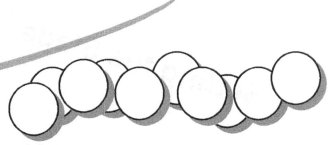

Answer Key

The tasks in which students decide what level of thinking is being used <u>always</u> stimulate active debate. This is intentional and desirable. If all items were easily classified, little new learning would take place. Depending on how students look at a task, they may argue that some low-level tasks are actually high-level and vice versa. For example, some students may perceive drama as a creative, high-level task. If the students were adding a new character to the story, creating a new scene, presenting a different ending or altering the story in some other fashion it would indeed be at the synthesis level. However, just acting out part of the story is no more sophisticated than writing a summary of the event or drawing a picture showing what happened in the story. Something new must be created mentally in order to qualify as synthesis.

Openly exploring the logic behind these opinions is precisely what you and your students should do. This answer key should only be used as a guideline. Welcome other responses that are well-reasoned and supported. Many other interpretations can be justified.

Task Cards
Low - Knowledge (recall) Give the names and dates of...
Low - Comprehension (retelling) Explain the term erode.
Medium - *Application (using a skill) Use the thesaurus...
Medium - *Application (demonstrate) Act out the final scene...
Medium - *Analysis (break down, investigate) Decide which size box...
Medium - *Analysis (examine, investigate) Determine how many hours...
High - Synthesis (imagine, adapt) Develop a new game....
High - Evaluation (rating, judging) Study the four clubhouse designs. Then choose...

*During discussions with students and teachers I have heard significant debate about the four items marked. While it seems like deciding which size box of detergent is the best deal is a basic compare and contrast task, students quickly demonstrated other equally justifiable answers. Example: Some students have questioned how well cheaper brands worked. What if you have to use twice as much to get things clean? Is that really the 'best" deal? What if it is double coupon day and the customer can save $1.00 on the more expensive brand?

Similar debates have occurred with the marigold task. It appears to be a straightforward science experiment. However on several occasions students have suggested that reading the planting instructions on the package would be a much better way to get the information and would be a low level task. Good point! So again, recognize that all thoughtful responses are to be accepted. Most tasks do not have one right answer. Let students listen to and learn from each other on all of the tasks. The answer keys are not absolute.

Setting the Stage

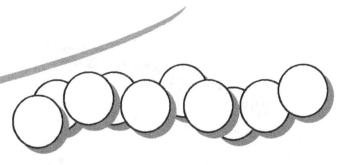

The acting task probably arouses the most debate. Drama can be a profoundly effective way to help students develop a deeper understanding of a novel. However, if all students do is pantomime or act out a scene, that does not require high-level thinking. It is no different than retelling the story or writing a summary — comprehension level tasks. Drama can only be classified as a synthesis-level task if it is done in a way which truly elicits high-level thinking. Having students respond to interview questions as if they are a key character, creating a new ending, or introducing a new problem for the characters to handle would be drama activities that qualify as high-level thinking. Please note the same arguments can apply if pictures are drawn. If the student simply shows a sequence of events, the thinking required isn't terribly sophisticated.

Many students and teachers feel the task in which a thesaurus is used requires high level thinking. In such cases they are viewing the revision process as extensive and thoughtful. Those thinking about it as simply using the thesaurus as a reference tool would classify the task at the application level.

Black Lagoon Tasks

Low - **Knowledge:** What equipment was used in the Media Center that is actually found in other businesses or industries?

Low - **Knowledge:** What was the librarian's name?

Medium - **Application:** Present a brief demonstration about the Dewey Decimal System.

Medium - **Analysis:** Find where the Library of Congress is located and how it is set up. Then explain why it is unique as compared to other libraries.

High - **Synthesis:** Use the following vocabulary words in a short story or radio advertisement: mortician, decontamination, pamphlet.

High - **Evaluation:** Why do you think the author chose to name the librarian's assistant Igor?

Mountain Bikes

Low - **Knowledge:** Jamie showed her father an ad for mountain bikes in the newspaper.

Low - **Comprehension:** Jamie told her father about the special features of the mountain bike.

Medium - **Analysis:** Jamie saw a second style of mountain bike she liked and carefully studied how it compared to the other one she was interested in.

Medium - **Application:** Jamie took the mountain bike for a test drive.

High - **Synthesis:** Jamie gave her father 37 reasons why he should split the cost of a new mountain bike with her.

High - **Evaluation:** Jamie asked the owner of the bike shop her opinion about different models of mountain bikes. Using this expert advice and information she'd collected earlier, Jamie then decided which bike to purchase.

12

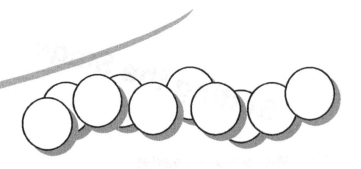

Setting the Stage

More than Anything Else

Low - **Knowledge**: What important gift does Mama give her son?

Low - **Comprehension**: How do the different members of the boy's family respond to his desire to read?

Medium - **Application**: Explain where salt comes from and how is it processed for use.

Medium - **Analysis**: Discuss the line "I have found hope, and it is as brown as me."

High - **Synthesis**: What kind of life experiences do you think might have prompted the author to create this book?

High - **Evaluation**: Choose three adjectives that clearly describe the main character. (Explain your choices.)

Sand Volleyball

Low - **Knowledge**: Little Boy Blue watched sand volleyball...

Low - **Comprehension**: Goldilocks explained the rules...

Medium - **Application**: Humpty Dumpty is taking...

Medium - **Analysis**: Doc and the other dwarves are carefully studying...

High - **Synthesis**: Red Riding Hood has designed a unique new...

High - **Evaluation**: Former gold medallists, Jack and Jill...

High - **Evaluation:** Kim tests new models of in-line skates...

Literature Task   (levels without modifications)

Low to Medium: Pick 3 key events from the story and act them out...

Low to Medium: Draw a cartoon of your favorite scene in the novel...

Low to Medium: List the difficult decisions facing the main characters in the story...

Low to Medium: Explain the meaning of the word *hyperbole.* Then use it in a sentence...

High: Select two passages you feel are clear examples of the author's writing style...

In-line Skating

Low - **Knowledge**: Kim shows her parents in-line skates...

Low - **Comprehension**: Kim explains to grandmother how in-line skates work...

Medium - **Application**: After completing a class...

Medium - **Analysis**: Kim is able to break down and copy moves...

High - **Synthesis**: Kim has developed several original new moves...

High - **Evaluation**: Kim tests new models of in-line skates...

13

Setting the Stage

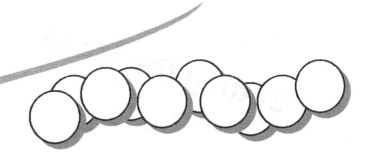

Take Me to Your Leader

Low - **Knowledge: Earnat** provided a basic description of candy, repeating the facts and information he has located.

Low - **Comprehenson: Korfutti** showed a better understanding of what candy is and also made an attempt to classify the various types.

Medium - **Application: Urrgoo** found out what candy is, sampled several kinds and is learning how it is made.

High - **Analysis: Galoop** studied the composition of candy, tasted it, and is breaking down and examining the specifics of its appeal to humans.

High - **Synthesis: Querk** applied the knowledge gained through research to make two kinds of candy humans prefer.

High - **Evaluation: Perdi** used a solid understanding of candy to create, test, and evaluate new treats that humans preferred over traditional favorites.

Cinderella

Low - **Knowledge**: What did the Fairy Godmother use...

Low - **Comprehension**: Describe how the different members of Cinderella's family...

Medium - **Application**: Act out the scene, or create a cartoon strip...

Medium - **Analysis**: Compare Cinderella's daily chores and responsibilities...

High - **Synthesis**: Set the Cinderella story in current times, or in another...

High - **Evaluation**: What kind of a message do you think...

Jets

Low - **Knowledge**: Cary can identify different...

Low - **Comprehension**: Cary can explain how...

Medium - **Application**: Cary is a jet pilot for...

Medium - **Analysis**: Cary has flown several different kinds...

High - **Synthesis**: Cary is a flight school instructor and recently...

High - **Evaluation**: Cary has been asked by the federal government...

14

Setting the Stage

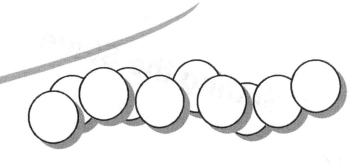

What You'll Need

	Individual Copies	Group Copies	Laminate for future use	Cut Apart
• Personal Reflections	X			
• Pyramid	X		X	
• In-line Skating	X			
• On Your Own	X			
• LMH rhyme		X		
• Task Cards		X	X	X
• Low, Medium, High strips		X	X	X
• Six Levels strips		X	X	X
• Mountain Bike		X		
• Sand Volleyball		X		
• Literature Tasks		X		
• Librarian from the Black Lagoon		X		
• More than Anything Else		X		
Optional Sheets				
• Take Me to Your Leader		X	X	X
• Cinderella	Individual	or group		
• Jets	individual	or group		

15

Setting the Stage

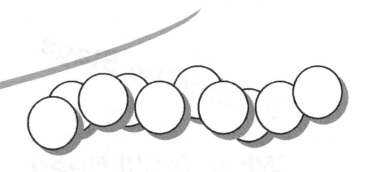

Name_____

Personal Reflections

1. Describe what you currently know about different kinds of thinking. If you don't really know anything about the topic just say so.

Date_____

---

2. Describe the new concepts you have learned related to different kinds of thinking.

3. How will this new knowledge affect your work in the future?

Date_____

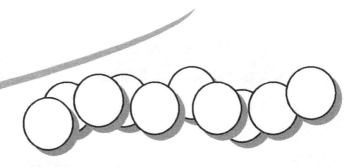

<u>Low</u>: I can list, name, describe, and explain.

<u>Medium</u>: I can use, solve, investigate, compare, contrast, or demonstrate.

<u>High</u>: I can design, invent, or create, judge, recommend, and rate.

17

Low

I can list, name, describe and explain.

Medium

I can use, solve, investigate, compare, contrast or demonstrate.

19

High

I can invent, design, or create, judge, recommend and rate.

20

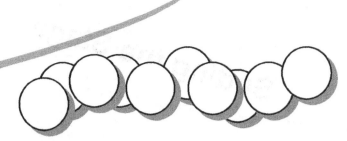

LMH Slips

Low
Medium
High

Setting the Stage

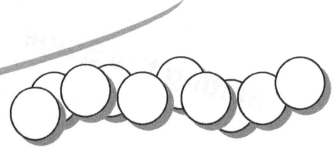

Task Cards

Cut apart the cards. Work with your team and sort them into tasks that require low, medium, and high levels of thinking. Be prepared to explain why you ranked each one as you did.

Use the thesaurus and rewrite the paragraph so it is more vivid and interesting.	**Act out the final scene from Goldilocks and the Three Bears.**
Determine how many hours of sunlight is best for growing marigolds.	**Study the four clubhouse designs. Choose the one you feel is best. Explain your reasons.**

22

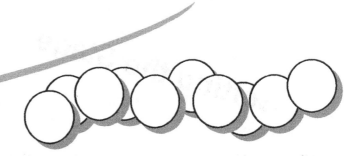

Decide which size box of detergent is the best deal.	Develop a new indoor recess game that uses a foam ball and music.
Explain what the term *erode* means.	Give the names and dates of three Confederate victories during the Civil War.

23

Setting the Stage

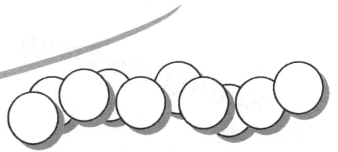

The Librarian from the Black Lagoon by Mike Thaler

Work with your group and analyze the level of thinking required by each question or task. Brainstorm ways to improve those you feel need to be stronger for use in lit circle discussions. (Hint: Low level questions with right and wrong answers don't leave much to discuss. Even just adding the word "why" can help elevate some questions.)

- What equipment was used in the Media Center that is actually found in other businesses or industries?

- What was the librarian's name?

- Present a brief demonstration about the Dewey Decimal System.

- Use the following vocabulary words in a short story or radio advertisement: mortician, decontamination, pamphlet.

- Why do you think the author chose to name the librarian's assistant Igor?

- Find where the Library of Congress is located and how it is set up. Then explain why it is unique as compared to other libraries.

24

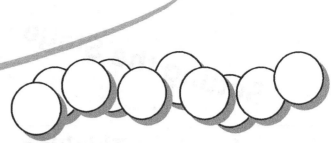

Mountain Bikes

Cut apart the cards. Work with your team and sort them into tasks that require low, medium and high levels of thinking. Be prepared to explain why you ranked each one as you did.

Jamie saw a second style of mountain bike she liked and studied it carefully to determine how it compared to the other one she was interested in.	Jamie asked the owner of the bike shop her opinion about different models of mountain bikes. Using this expert advice and information she'd collected earlier, Jamie decided which bike to purchase.
Jamie gave her father 37 different reasons why he should split the cost of a new mountain bike with her.	Jamie test drove a popular style of mountain bike.
Jamie showed her father an ad for mountain bikes in the newspaper.	Jamie told her father about the features of the mountain bike.

25

Setting the Stage

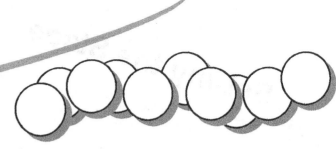

Levels of Thinking Pyramid based on Bloom's Taxonomy

judge

conclude

interpret

Evaluation
To Justify

adapt   hypothesize   imagine

Synthesis
To Create or Change

examine   **Analysis**   break down
             To Examine
compare/contrast   investigate

demonstrate   **Application**   apply
                 To Use
organize   solve   do

paraphrase   **Comprehension**   explain
                To Understand
interpret   describe

recognize   **Knowledge**   tell   remember
list   *To Recall*

26

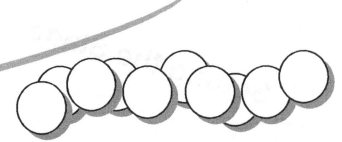

Six Levels

Knowledge
Comprehension
Application

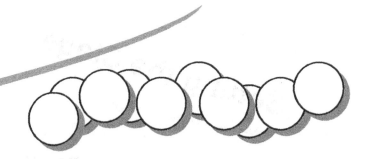

Analysis

Synthesis

Evaluation

Setting the Stage

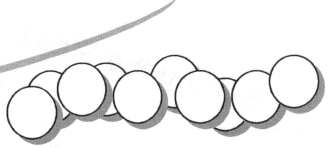

More Than Anything Else by Marie Bradby

Work with your group and analyze the level of thinking required by each question or task. Brainstorm ways to improve those you feel need to be stronger for use in lit circle discussions. (Hint: Low level questions with right and wrong answers don't leave much to discuss. Even just adding the word "why" can help elevate some questions.)

- What kind of life experiences do you think might have prompted the author to create this book?

- Choose three quality adjectives that are not in the book that describe the main character. Be prepared to explain your choices.

- Explain where salt comes from and how it is processed for use.

- What important gift does Mama give her son?

- Discuss the beauty and meaning of the line "I have found hope, and it is as brown as me."

- How do the different members of the boy's family respond to his desire to read?

29

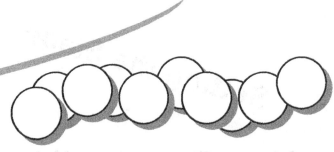

Name_____   Date_____

Sand Volleyball

1. Write the most appropriate level of thinking next to each item below.
2. Explain your decisions on the back of the paper. (Hint: focus on key verbs that reflect what kind of thinking was involved.)

_____Former gold medallists, Jack and Jill, are coaches for the National Sand Volleyball Team.

_____Little Boy Blue watched sand volleyball on television for the first time last Saturday.

_____Red Riding Hood has designed a unique new defensive strategy for her sand volleyball team.

_____Goldilocks explained the rules of sand volleyball during her presentation in public speaking class.

_____Doc and the other dwarves are carefully studying tapes of their opponents in the upcoming sand volleyball tournament so they understand the teams' strengths and weaknesses.

_____Humpty Dumpty is taking his first sand volleyball class at summer camp.

Setting the Stage

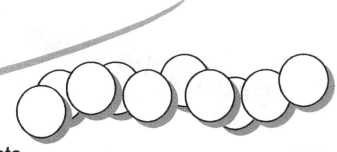

Names_____ Date_____

Literature Tasks

Think carefully about the tasks and questions below. First, list the level of thinking required by each one. Although there is nothing wrong with any of them, each could be strengthened. Next, use what you know about higher-level thinking and suggest a simple way to improve the items. Last, describe the level of thinking required by each of your revised tasks.

Example: Discuss how the main character has matured or changed. _Analysis_

Why did these changes take place and what impact might they have on the character in the future? Evaluation

1. Pick 3 key events from the story and act them out. _____

2. Draw a cartoon of your favorite scene in the novel. _____

3. List the difficult decisions facing the main characters in the story. _____

4. Explain the meaning of the word *hyperbole*. Then use it in a sentence. _____

5. Select two passages you feel are clear examples of the author's writing style. _____

31

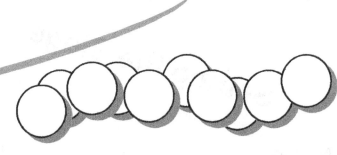

Name_____ **Date**_____

In-line Skating

1. Write the most appropriate level of thinking next to each item below.
2. Explain your decisions on the back of the paper. (Hint: focus on key verbs that reflect what kind of thinking was required to perform each task.)

_____ A recent issue of *Sports Illustrated for Kids* featured an article about Kim. She has developed several original new moves that have taken in-line skating in a new direction.

_____ Kim shows her parents the in-line skates and safety equipment at the sporting goods store.

_____ After completing a class through the park district, Kim uses basic in-line skating techniques and safety measures.

_____ Kim is able to break down and then copy moves used by top-ranked in-line skating athletes.

_____ Kim tests new models of in-line skates and safety equipment for a major manufacturer. She provides specific feedback to help the designers improve the performance of the new products.

_____ Kim explains to her grandmother how in-line skates work and how they are different from traditional roller skates.

Setting the Stage

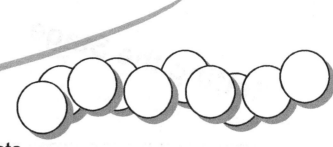

Names_____   Date_____

On Your Own

Develop six questions or tasks related to a story. Have them represent all levels of thinking. Be prepared to explain what level you feel each one reflects. Record that information on a separate piece of paper.

1.

2.

3.

4.

5.

6.

33

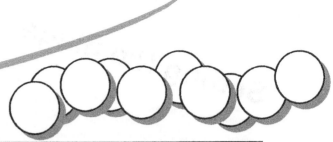

Take Me To Your Leader

Phase One

To: Advisors of the High Council of Zoargut
From: The Most High Poobah

The High Council is in the process of selecting a new Chief of Exploration. As Council Advisors, you will work together and rank the six candidates for the position. Before you can judge the finalists, you must understand the rating system being used to evaluate each creature's thinking.

Many different levels of thinking are used to handle the information and decisions we face each day. Bloom's Taxonomy is one system used to describe those different levels of thought.

In Phase One of your mission, you and your team must develop an understanding of Bloom's Taxonomy. During Phase Two, you will apply what you have learned as you evaluate reports submitted by candidates for the position of Chief of Exploration.

To Do...

1. Carefully study the six levels of thinking in Bloom's Taxonomy. Think about the key words associated with each level.
2. Work together and place the cards in order from the most basic level of thinking to the most complex.
3. Be ready to explain your team's decisions.
4. Once you have satisfactorily completed your Phase One training, you will be given permission to advance to Phase Two and rate the candidates for Chief of Exploration.

34

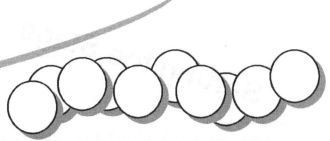

Take Me To Your Leader

Phase Two

As advisors to the High Council of Zoargut, you must assist in the selection of the new Chief of Exploration for your planet. Six candidates have been sent to Earth as part of a leadership training seminar. How they perform on this mission will decide which one is appointed Chief.

Their mission is to investigate and report on the immensely popular Earth substance "candy." As advisors to the High Council, you are responsible for rating the quality of thinking exhibited in each report using Bloom's Taxonomy as your guide.

To Do...

1. Work with your team and match each report to the corresponding level in Bloom's. Our initial examination indicates there is one report at each level.
2. Explain what level of thinking you feel is exhibited in each report. Describe why you gave each report the rating you did.
3. Be prepared to explain your decisions to the full council.

Hint: Use the Bloom's Taxonomy cards to help accurately evaluate each candidate's report. Focus on the key words that go with each level. Examine just what kind of thinking each creature demonstrated.

35

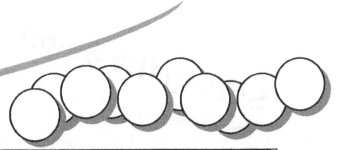

Final Report for the High Council

Creature	What level did you place the creature at and why?

36

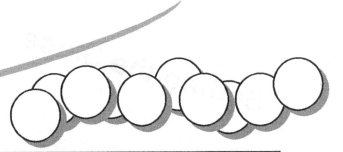

Final Recommendation for the High Council

Write a paragraph in which you describe the creature you recommend for the position of Chief of Exploration. List the specific reasons why you feel this creature is the best candidate for the job.

37

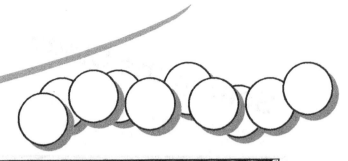

Most High Poobah,

Determining the composition of candy and learning how it is made were relatively simple tasks. Even after tasting different kinds of candy myself, I had unanswered questions. Therefore, I have beamed a group of Earthlings aboard my vessel to determine:

1. Exactly why do humans crave candy?
2. What makes particular flavors so appealing?

Galoop

Most High Poobah,

I used a number of research tools to determine the ingredients found in candy. I have chemical formulas for those most commonly used. I am now trying to organize and sort the different types of candy available. My research shows that humans mostly buy candy at stores and gas stations. Some use special formulas and make it at home.

Korfutti

38

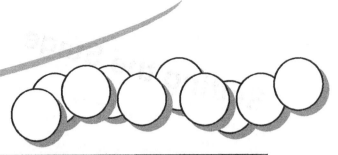

Most High Poobah,

I have investigated the availability and composition of countless kinds of candy. I sampled several varieties: candy bars, hard candies, and chewy candies. I am still studying a strange type of candy called gum. By assuming human form, I got a job at a company which manufactures candy. When I return to our planet, I will demonstrate how it is made.

Urrgoo

Most High Poobah,

Based on my careful research and far-reaching investigation, I know the most common ingredients used to produce candy. I also know how humans acquire it. Although I didn't find many kinds of candy personally tasty, humans clearly love it. I used shipping and sales records to determine the most popular kinds of candy. At this time I am copying the formulas for the two top-selling varieties.

Querk

39

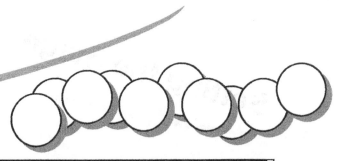

Most High Poobah,

I now know exactly what the substance called candy is. By using candy wrappers, a dictionary and chemistry textbooks, I have compiled a list of ingredients used to create candy. Basically it is a sweet food made from sugar or syrup. It can include ingredients such as chocolate, nuts, and fruit. I found it also frequently included a number of chemicals and preservatives.

Earnat

Most High Poobah,

I have carefully studied and consumed a wide variety of candies. I have tracked human consumption patterns, likes and dislikes. Using all that information, I have developed and tested my own candy formulas on human subjects. My formulas have proven quite successful. Earthlings would rather eat my candy than watch TV, play, sleep, or be with their loved ones!

Perdi

40

Setting the Stage

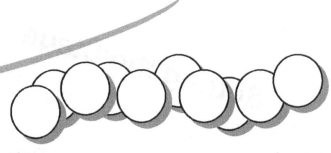

Name_____ Date_____

Cinderella

1. Write the most appropriate level of thinking next to each item below.
2. Explain your decisions on the back of the paper. (Hint: focus on key verbs that reflect what kind of thinking was involved.)

_____ Set the Cinderella story in current times or in another culture. The influence of this new setting should be evident in your writing.

_____ Compare Cinderella's daily chores and responsibilities with those you have at your home.

_____ Describe how the various members of Cinderella's family treated her.

_____ What kind of a message do you think the Cinderella story sends to young girls? What are your thoughts about this?

_____ What did the Fairy Godmother use for a carriage?

_____ Act out the scene or create a cartoon strip showing Cinderella getting ready for the ball.

Setting the Stage

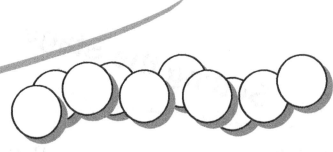

Name_____ Date_____

Jets

1. Write the most appropriate level of thinking next to each item below.
2. Explain your decisions on the back of the paper. (Hint: focus on key verbs that reflect what kind of thinking was involved.)

_____ Cary has flown several different kinds of jets and can explain how they compare.

_____ Cary can explain how jets fly.

_____ Cary is a jet pilot for a major airline.

_____ Cary has been asked by the federal government to direct the Federal Aviation Administration. In this new role, Cary is responsible for over-seeing major changes in how pilots are trained and licensed.

_____ Cary is a flight school instructor and recently designed a new technique to help make emergency landings safer.

_____ Cary can identify different kinds of jets.

42

Dynamic Sharing Tools for Lit Circles

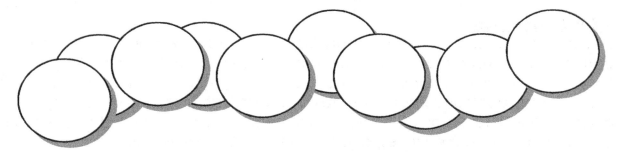

* Structuring and Managing Lit Circles
* 12 Easy-to-Create Sharing Tools
* Visual Aids, Drama, and Games to explore Characters, Conflicts, Setting, Vocabulary and Author's Craft

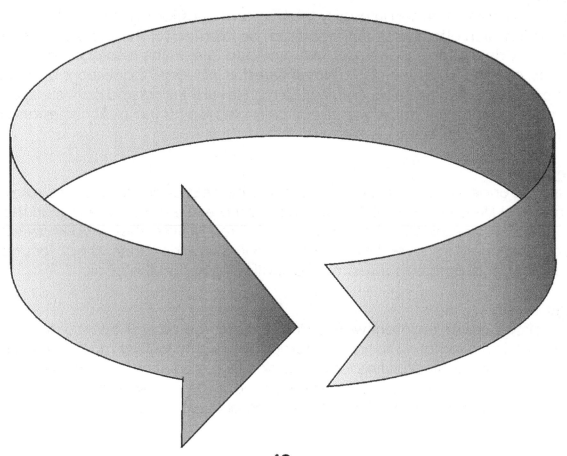

43

Teacher Background

A Solid Foundation

Literature circles can inspire top quality discussion and thinking in ways no other approach can match. Passionate debates emerge and even reluctant readers plunge into the action. However, this only happens if students are thoroughly prepared before working in lit circles. If they don't understand how to engage in high-level thinking and questioning, the quality of their interaction will be ho-hum to poor at best. Because of this, learners won't be adequately prepared to respond thoughtfully to top-level questions posed by the teacher.

If you are certain the learners in your room are ready to consistently use high-level thinking with lit circle sharing tools, proceed with confidence! Otherwise, spend a week laying a solid foundation before moving on. The time will be well worth it. **Setting the Stage** provides step-by-step plans and hands-on activities to directly teach students about high-level thinking.

Sharing Tools

Once students are well versed in quality thinking and questioning, expose them to a variety of ways in which effective sharing tools can be created for the various lit circle roles. Instructions for developing twelve tools are provided later in this resource. To give students more ideas, consider using the game **Novel Quest**. It includes 70 questions and challenges that serve as additional examples. All require high-level thinking and active engagement from group members. The game was specifically created for use by lit circles and is designed to work with any book.

Accountability

Students must understand your expectations and be held accountable for exploring all the elements of literature you require. So whether the entire class is working on the same novel, or students are selecting from a variety of different titles, they must know what key areas you want them to cover through their activities. You can then check for understanding on an individual basis with assessment activities related to the book.

Grouping

Literature circles are an excellent way to differentiate. Therefore, how you structure them is important. While it is tempting to have heterogeneous groups, that may pose problems in terms of pacing. If one student finishes the book in two days, and the others have ten chapters left, it won't be a successful learning experience. Likewise, one title may not be at the appropriate reading level for all of the learners in your room.

What Kind of Books

Choose novels with strong student appeal that match the needs and interests of your students. Selecting books for which learners can't muster any enthusiasm is a recipe for disaster. If you want to use a "classic," wait until students are highly skilled at operating in lit circles before doing so. What you choose must provide appropriate challenge for the different reading levels present in your classroom. One size does not fit all. There may be a time when you want every student reading the same novel. When this is the case, be sure to allow highly capable readers to move at a more rapid pace. Likewise, provide additional support for less able readers. Those finishing early can read another book by the same author, on the same theme, or choose an extension project to complete from options you provide.

How Many Titles

If this is the first time students are using sharing tools driven by high-level thinking, working with one novel is a good plan. The structure is reassuring to both teachers and students. If you have learners select from an array of books, the **Novel Selection Sheet** provides a simple way to organize their choices. Present a two-minute sales pitch for each selection available. Have students indicate their reading pace and top three choices. Use this information, along with your professional judgment, to form four-person lit circles.

Assessment Options with Multiple Titles

Since students produce the actual discussion activities, using different novels simultaneously is manageable. Try using books with a common theme. If you chose survival books at a range of reading levels, your individual assessments would include common elements of such novels. If you elect to use three or four different titles at once, use generic questions and tasks that explore important aspects of novels such as conflicts, characters, theme, or the author's craft. This method allows students reading different books to respond to identical questions. Developing a list of such questions with your students also gives them a tool to use should a group member be absent on sharing day. If you have the time and energy, use assessments targeted to each specific book.

Whichever route you choose, select your groups, novels, and assessment tools with care. And regardless which books or grouping strategies you use, remember that your interaction with the readers is essential. Sit down and play part of an activity with a group. Periodically interject questions of your own for discussion. Both approaches help you monitor student progress and understanding.

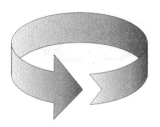

Paperwork

Paperwork can become overwhelming in this profession. When using lit circles avoid the temptation to micromanage. There is no need to collect letter grades each time students have discussions. As you rotate around the room, just carry a clipboard and a checklist. Note which students are fully engaged and identify learners that need additional coaching. A simple rubric has been included in this resource. It enables you and the students to evaluate the effectiveness of sharing tools and group discussions.

Although sheets have been provided for each lit circle role (visual, discussion, drama, and vocabulary) they are entirely optional. Many teachers don't feel the need to use them once students are competent at executing the various roles. You may want to periodically collect a written description about your students' sharing tools.

Skill Levels

It takes time, practice, and feedback to become proficient at developing and using high quality sharing tools. Some students advance very rapidly. Others remain at the novice or developing levels for some time.

- **Novice** - The entire class develops tools designed to fulfill the same literature circle role (visual, discussion, drama, and vocabulary). This works well when first introducing powerful sharing tools. For example, have all students create visual tools to extend thinking about the novel. After trying them out in small groups, share and evaluate them as a class. The focus should be on the effectiveness of each tool. Did it keep all group members actively involved? Did it elicit high-level thinking? If the tool failed on either count, have the class brainstorm how to modify it for future use. You may work with low readers in your room at this level indefinitely.
- **Developing** - Once students have some experience, allow those ready to move on to work together in small teams and develop tools for one particular role. Mix members of the various groups to create lit circles in which all four roles are represented.
- **Expert** - Many students will soon be ready to independently create sharing tools for use within their circles. To keep new ideas alive, periodically have students explain new tools to the rest of the class.

Getting Started

Every classroom is different, so instructing teachers to follow an identical recipe for introducing sharing tools is difficult. The following procedure is one tried and true approach. Your path may be longer or shorter. Some students may progress more rapidly than others. Just take it in manageable steps so neither you nor the students become overwhelmed. In time you will develop tools and routines that work successfully for you.

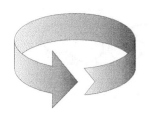

Step 1	Step 2	Step 3	Step 4
Read a quality picture book to the class. Prepare 2 sharing tools for students to complete in groups of 3 or 4. Discuss level of thinking and quality of interaction each tool elicits after students have used them.	Read a 2nd quality picture book to the class. Prepare 2 new sharing tools for students to complete in groups of 3 or 4. Repeat the tool analysis discussion.	Read a 3rd quality picture book to the class. Have each group of 3 or 4 students work together to create or use a new sharing tool. Each student makes a copy of the tool and then uses it with a new mixed discussion group.	Have students return to their tool-making group to compare results and adjust the tool as needed. Then ask each team to share their tool with the class, describing how it worked and what if any improvements are needed.

Step 5	Step 6	Step 7	Step 8
Read a final quality picture book to the class. Using new groupings, have students repeat steps 3 and 4.	Have students develop a list briefly describing those tools used so far that meet the guidelines on the rubric. This helps them remember options they can create for future lit circles.	Begin using an actual novel or story. Based on your observations of their readiness, have students work independently, in pairs or with you to develop/use sharing tools for their first lit circle. Some may be ready to create original tools.	As students are ready, move them from novice to developing to expert levels. Be sure they work with others at a similar level of readiness so both the pace and the level of reading material provide the appropriate amount of challenge.

Initially, many teachers elect to have a small group of the most capable readers continue after step two. While other students read or complete seatwork, the teacher coaches this pilot group through the rest of the progression. They can then demonstrate their tools for the class. Gradually as other students are ready, launch them into the process. Some may never create tools independently, but they still benefit from using those which promote top-quality discussion that the teacher creates.

Remember...modeling, sharing, and non-threatening feedback are essential. Without such practices students won't learn to create and use truly effective sharing tools which promote insightful discussions.

Tips on Upgrading Tools

When first using drama, many students simply act out events from the story. Unfortunately, that task is only at the comprehension level. Using higher-level thinking skills, thus improving the tool, the actors could share the character's inner thoughts. Perhaps three different conflicts could be acted out. Afterwards the group could rank them in order of their importance to the overall plot. If a visual tool didn't offer enough different class discussion or if it was too literal (a toy tractor represented exactly that), brainstorm with the class. Help students explore ways more symbolic items could spark deeper discussions. For example, in a survival novel, a stick could represent shelter, a weapon, being lost in the woods, attempts to build a fire, or symbolize a character's growing inner strength.

Problems

What about students who are disruptive or unprepared? Once students experience the excitement of using well-crafted sharing tools and high-level thinking to explore compelling books, many behavior problems are controlled. If you have students who are consistently unprepared or off-task, give them more structured reading activities to complete independently.

Student Routines and Responsibilities

Work with your students through the sheets provided to help them understand your expectations. Provide opportunities to develop, share, and reflect on tools for various lit circle roles. Don't grade their initial efforts. Give feedback in a non-threatening way as their skills develop.

Remember

Many educators just like you have stepped back from their current reading practices, taught their students how to be quality thinkers, and embraced this approach to literature circles. Our experiences, teacher feedback, and responses from students have helped us develop a powerful and simple way for learners to get the most out of their discussions. The provided plan is flexible. Each classroom, every teacher and student is different so . . .

- Pick appropriate novels that will excite students and stimulate discussion.
- Experiment with how you assign roles and conduct literature circle activities.
- Develop a resource binder of "generic" ideas that can work with any novel.
- Save samples of powerful sharing tools.
- Video your students explaining and using sharing tools to show to other classes.
- Regularly reflect with your learners about what you have achieved. Then refine your efforts to improve future results.
- Invite parents to read the same novels as their students and join you for a lit circle luncheon. There is no better way to help parents appreciate and understand this powerful instructional approach.

The Sharing Tools

The tools described in this resource are starting points for your students. These particular activities stimulate quality thinking and discussion while actively engaging all group members. All are simple to make and use. Encourage students to develop their own creative sharing tools as soon as they are ready. Just be sure they follow the guidelines on the rubric.

Novel Selection Sheet

Name_____

Circle the speed at which you normally read a novel such as those described by the teacher.

13+ days   10-12 days   7-9 days   4-6 days   1-3 days

Choice 1_____

Choice 2 _____

Choice 3 _____

Additional Information

To the Student — Routines and Responsibilities

To Begin

When starting a new novel, take the first few minutes of class to plan a reasonable reading and job schedule. Because the length of chapters can vary widely, it is usually best to determine about how many pages your group will read each day. If the entire class is reading the same book, the teacher will work with you to determine the schedule. If your team is reading its own book, submit a copy of your reading and job schedule to the teacher for approval. Then update your assignment notebooks accordingly. You may need to adjust your schedule if your original pace was either too ambitious or too slow.

Before you begin reading, divide the book and have each member skim one or two chapters in search of new vocabulary words. Your combined list should have a total of 8-12 quality words that would improve your writing and speaking. Have each person look up the definition, part of speech, and pronunciation of his/her words. Write an example sentence for each word. Use the Vocabulary Chart provided, or type it on a computer. The teacher and each group member needs a copy. Use this list throughout the novel for all vocabulary activities. Study it a few minutes each day <u>before</u> meeting together in your lit circle.

Responsibilities & Evaluation

Literature circles meet about three or four times during the course of a novel. Use the length of the book and the number of days you have to complete it to guide your planning. Rotate job assignments each time. About once a week you will take a quiz or complete an independent activity for a letter grade. The work you and your partners do in your literature circle should help prepare you for this. Eventually the quality of your sharing tools and participation in the circle discussions will be evaluated. If your group has a member who consistently fails to follow through with his/her responsibilities, ask your teacher for guidance. That student may need to work independently.

In a literature circle, other team members are depending on your best efforts. Don't let them down. Demonstrate courtesy, responsibility, and respect by completing your particular task on time and in a quality manner. If you regularly have difficulty keeping up with the group, discuss the situation with your teacher. Help absent students by carefully reviewing with them what you developed. Remember, sharing the work load is much better than having to do it alone. One last tip - while it is **always** ok to read ahead, be courteous and think before you speak. Revealing upcoming events ruins the book for the other readers.

The Roles

Discussion activities should take the group about 15-20 minutes to complete. Other tools should involve circle members for approximately 10 minutes each. Regardless which role you have in a literature circle, you must be prepared to explain how your tool works and what level of thinking it requires. Remember, the goal for every tool is to stimulate quality thinking and discussion. Some activities simply work better than others. If yours needs adjusting once you begin using it, gracefully accept suggestions from your group.

Guidelines for Creating Tools

- **A tool should usually take 20 minutes or less to create.**
- **It needs to actively involve all of the group members. So watch out that there isn't too much "down" time when one player is busy and the others have to sit and wait.**
- **It must require members to engage in high levels of thinking. (*application level or above*)**
- **The tools tend to overlap and may involve many different elements. For example, a discussion activity could also involve the use of drama. Visual tools always involve discussion. Crossovers like that are fine.**

Sharing Tools for Literature Circles

Name_____   Date_____

Features	1, 2 or 3 Below Expectations	4, 5 or 6 Meets Expectations	7, 8 or 9 Exceeds Expectations
The tool enabled all circle members to actively participate.			
The tool required participants to consistently use medium to high levels of thinking.			
The tool was created in 20 minutes or less.			
The group worked together effectively to explore the assigned reading.			

Comments:

Vocabulary Chart

Word	Part of Speech	Pronunciation	Record the definition & two synonyms for the word.

On the back of the sheet, write a sample sentence using each vocabulary word.

Lit Circle Schedule

Days → Tasks ⬇					
Assigned Reading					
Discussion Master					
Vocabulary Master					
Visual Master					
Drama Master					

Comments regarding the team's performance/progress:

Visual Tools

<u>Visual Master</u> – Visual prompts are an excellent way to get members of the group to explore the assigned reading. This is **not** show-and-tell time for the visual piece you create! Make sure others get to respond to, or even help fill in the tool. If their ideas are different from yours, that is fine. It gives everyone new ways to think about the book. Comparing and contrasting characters, ranking the importance of key conflicts, or focusing on the setting are excellent areas to explore visually.

<u>1. Charts and Diagrams</u>

Develop a chart for the group to complete about significant ways in which two characters are alike and different. Categories should include a variety of areas such as:

Characters	Hillary	Sarah-Kate
Strengths		
Weaknesses		
Beliefs		
Personality		
Social/Cultural Background		
Physical Appearance		

Your task is to create the chart or diagram. The actual content should be filled in by the group during your part of the lit circle discussion.

<u>2. Character Bubbles</u>

Create very simple sketches of three key events or conflicts in the story. Make conversation bubbles for each character shown in the drawings. When you work in your circle, have the group members share what they think the characters were thinking or feeling at that point in the novel.

Characters	Strengths	Weaknesses	Beliefs	Personality	Social/Cultural Background	Physical Appearance

3. Graphic Organizer

Use Sherlock to guide your discussion about the main characters. Explore each of the seven aspects shown. Record the four key ideas that caused the most lively discussion among members of the group.

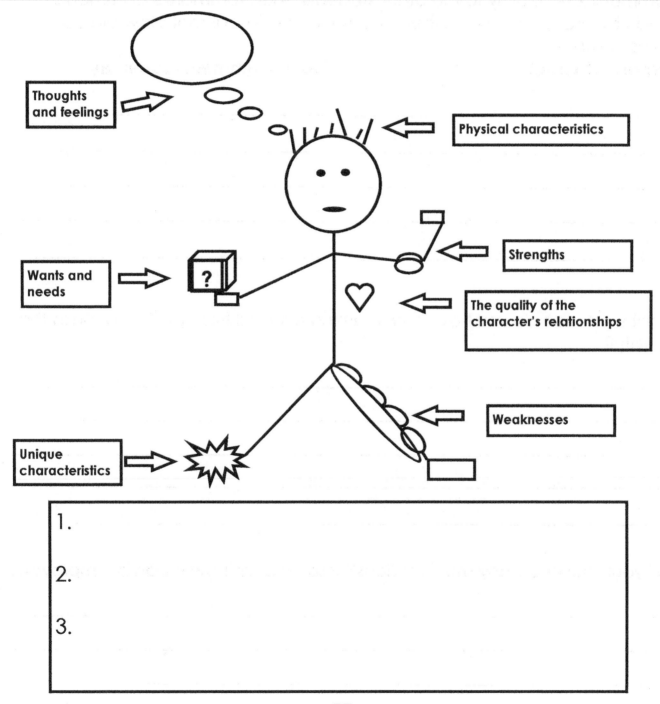

Thoughts and feelings

Physical characteristics

Wants and needs

Strengths

The quality of the character's relationships

Unique characteristics

Weaknesses

1.

2.

3.

*Dynamic Sharing
Tools for Lit Circles*

Visual Master _____   Date_____

Write a brief paragraph that explains your work and what you intended to communicate visually to the other students. Then summarize comments made by group members when discussing your visual tool. How did your ideas compare?

Purpose of Visual   **Group Comments Summary**

_____   _____

_____   _____

_____   _____

_____   _____

_____   _____

What evidence do you have that learning resulted from participation in the activity?

_____

_____

_____

_____

_____

Did your tool need any modifications? If so, explain how it can be improved.

_____

_____

_____

Drama Tools

Drama Master – Your mission is to use drama as a way to get the other group members actively thinking at high levels about the characters, vocabulary, conflicts, and events in the novel. Some students just want to act out scenes from the book. This only requires low-level thinking, so you'll need to push beyond that.

1. Sharing Passages

Select three special passages that are thought provoking, funny, informative, moving, descriptive, or even confusing. Mark the places with slips of paper. Have group members read the passages aloud. If a selection includes dialogue, the students can play the parts of the different characters.

Stop and discuss the passages from different perspectives. For example, the group could explore how the writer created powerful descriptions of the setting or of a character. Discuss the inner thoughts or feelings of characters that might not have been directly expressed in the book. Talk about how an event you read relates to your lives, or connects to the real world in some fashion. Your job is to mark the passages and write the discussion questions. Share your comments after the others have had a chance to speak.

2. Charades Sequence Game

Create 6-8 cards with key conflicts or events from the novel written on them. Players take turns selecting a card and silently acting out the scene while others guess what is going on. Once the right answer is given, place the card face-up in a time line. Each event is then placed in the correct sequence as it is guessed. Once all of the cards are in order, discuss which three had the most significant impact on the main character and why.

Tink gets cancer and John learns what lies ahead.	Young John prepares for his summer alone.	Show all of the disasters on John's first day.	The sheep dogs require special care.	John eats "mystery meals".	John's father finally talks about the past.

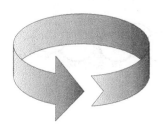

3. New Conversations

Use two slips of paper to mark places in the novel where:

1. You wish you could talk directly to the character or ask him or her questions about their feelings and actions.

2. You wish the main characters would have a conversation, but the author didn't include one in the book.

Share the two passages. For task one, have one person pretend to be the character while others ask him or her relevant questions about his or her feelings and actions in that part of the book.

For the second task, select two people to become the characters. They should have the unwritten conversation. Other group members can ask them questions once they are finished.

Drama Master_____   Date_____

In a brief paragraph, explain how drama was used to extend thinking about the book.

_____

_____

_____

_____

_____

_____

What evidence do you have that learning resulted from participation in the activity?

_____

_____

_____

_____

Did your tool need any modifications? If so, explain how it can be improved.

_____

_____

_____

_____

_____

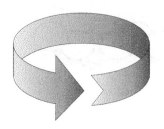 

Vocabulary Tools

Vocabulary Master -

It is most successful if all students are given a list of vocabulary words and definitions before starting a novel. That allows the Vocabulary Master to focus on creating activities in which students use the words in speaking and writing.

Students should not be seeing new vocabulary for the first time when the group gathers for sharing activities. One practice that works well is dividing up the entire novel, giving each student a chapter or two in which to search for new words. The goal is to select words they can realistically use to enhance their speaking and writing.

Students write down 3 words, the part of speech and the most appropriate definition for each. They also create an example sentence for each one. This information is given to the teacher and he or she develops the final vocabulary list from the "nominated" words.

Your job involves finding creative and effective methods that help other students **use** the new vocabulary words correctly. Just matching the words and their definitions isn't enough. Members should already be familiar with the words since they are from the vocabulary sheet for the unit. Be sure you play along with your group.

1. Guess that Word

This 4-person game is played in pairs. Place each vocabulary word on 2 separate cards. Player one from Team A and Player one from Team B take those matching cards. They take turns giving their partners one-word clues that should help him or her guess which word is being used. Play alternates back and forth until the word is guessed. The player that got the right answer must then correctly use the word in a sentence. Clue givers and their partners trade jobs after each round. Since you get information from both your partner and from the clue given to the opposing team, careful listening is essential. Look at the example game below for the word "distressed".

Player A: "Upset"   Partner's response: "Annoyed"
Player B: "Disturbed"   Partner's response: "Distressed"

2. Instant Commercial

Place each vocabulary word on a separate card. Have someone select three cards and turn them face-up for the group to see. Working in pairs, take three minutes and write a 30-second commercial for a product of your choice. Use all three words correctly in your ad. Perform the commercials for each other. This example uses *flustered, meander* and *courageous.*

"There are so many kinds of toothpaste. Do all those choices leave you feeling <u>flustered</u> and confused? Don't just <u>meander</u> up and down the isles muttering to yourself. Be <u>courageous</u> and try Scrubbing Bubble Toothpaste today. It may taste like bathtub cleanser, but boy does it make your teeth shine!"

3. Triple Concentration

Choose 6 vocabulary words you can foresee using when speaking and writing. Cut a large piece of construction paper into 18 small cards. Write each vocabulary word on a card. Put the definition for each word on a different card. On a third card, find or draw an image that clearly relates to the word. Mix the 18 cards and place facedown for a game of Triple Concentration.

Players turn 3 cards face up. The object of the game is to find the word, definition and matching image. Once a 3-way match is found, the player must correctly use the word in a sentence in order to keep the set.

studious	Devoted to study. Earnest, diligent.	

"Thanks to her careful analysis, the studious young woman made a fortune in the stock market."

63

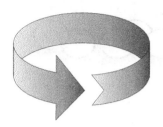

Vocabulary Master_____ Date_____

In a brief paragraph, explain how you helped group members learn to use the new vocabulary words.

_____

_____

_____

_____

_____

_____

What evidence do you have that learning resulted from participation in the activity?

_____

_____

_____

_____

Did your tool need any modifications? If so, explain how it can be improved.

_____

_____

_____

_____

_____

_____

Discussion Tools

Discussion Master – Your job is to create an activity that stimulates high quality thinking and discussion about various aspects of the novel. The tool must actively involve all group members. This is **not** the place for questions with right or wrong answers.

1. Board Game
- Create a game board using construction paper. Draw at least 15-20 spaces on which the tokens can move.
- Remember, the purpose of the game is to stimulate quality discussion.
- Make cards for conflicts, characters, setting and vocabulary. Label the spaces on the board to match the task cards the players will draw during the game.
- Put no more than 3 penalty spaces on the board such as "Go back 3 spaces" or "Loose a turn."
- Develop tasks or questions at the application level or higher for the cards. Make 4 or 5 cards of each type.
- Gather dice or make a spinner. Use tokens from other games or make simple ones from small slips of paper. Keep the rules simple.
- After the player drawing a card responds, others should share their ideas too. As the discussion master, save your comments for last each time.

2. Mystery Objects
Select 6-8 items that represent some aspect of the novel and place them in a brown lunch bag or a box. The things you include should be symbolic and have more than one possible meaning or interpretation. For example, something as simple as a stick could represent shelter, a weapon, being lost in the woods, or even a character's growing inner strength. Include items that deal with the characters, conflicts, vocabulary, setting, key events and even the author. Players take turns drawing an object from the bag and sharing how it could relate to the novel. Pass the objects around the group in order to hear other possible connections. As the discussion master, save your comments for last each time.

3. Happy Holidays

Choose two key characters from the book. During the next 3 minutes, list four gifts you feel would be suitable for each one. Have each group member share their gift ideas. Others should guess why they think each choice was made. After exploring the reasons, each member then reveals why he or she selected the gifts they did. Make selections that are symbolic. For example, give the villain in a novel a new vacuum so he can "clean up his act". Perhaps having a video camera would enable a character to solve a central conflict being faced in the story.

Character 1 _____	Character 2 _____
Gift 1:	Gift 1:
Reason	Reason
Gift 2:	Gift 2:
Reason	Reason
Gift 3:	Gift 3:
Reason	Reason
Gift 4:	Gift 4:
Reason	Reason

Discussion Master_____   Date_____

In a brief paragraph, explain how your activity worked. Describe what aspects of the novel it helped the group explore.

_____

_____

_____

_____

_____

_____

_____

What evidence do you have that learning resulted from participation in the activity?

_____

_____

_____

_____

Did your tool need any modifications? If so, explain how it can be improved.

_____

_____

_____

Novel Quest

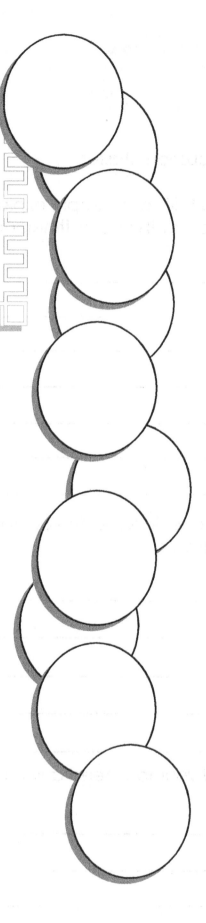

Ready-to-go Game for Exploring Literature for
4-6 players

70 high-level Questions & Instant Challenges
explore Character, Setting, Plot, Conflict &
Author's Craft

NOVEL QUEST

This game is a powerful tool for stimulating quality thinking and discussion for groups of 3 to 5 students and can be used with any story. It also gives students more than 70 examples of high-level questions and tasks they can adapt for use in future lit circle activities they develop.

Make copies of the four-part game board, spinner, and question cards to create enough kits for your classroom. To save time, laminate the items and store in large envelopes for future use.

69

How to Play

Players   3-5

Materials   4 sections of game board taped together, tokens, spinner, question cards, scratch paper, and pencils

To Play   Place tokens on **Start**. Put the cards on top of the sheet provided. Follow the instructions on the spinner. Take a card from the stack with the same shape and do what it says. After that player has responded to the question or task, others may add their ideas.

There are generally no "wrong" answers in Novel Quest. Since the game stimulates quality thinking and discussion, every player wins. Play concludes when the last player reaches the finish.

The Goal of Novel Quest is to stimulate quality thinking and discussion so players benefit from hearing the viewpoints and insights of others. There are generally no "wrong" answers in Novel Quest, but all responses should be supported with reasons and examples as required. After playing, students should feel prepared to independently answer questions about the novel. The game also provides a wealth of ideas that can be used to craft quality questions for sharing tools in future lit circle discussions.

70

START

Novel

71

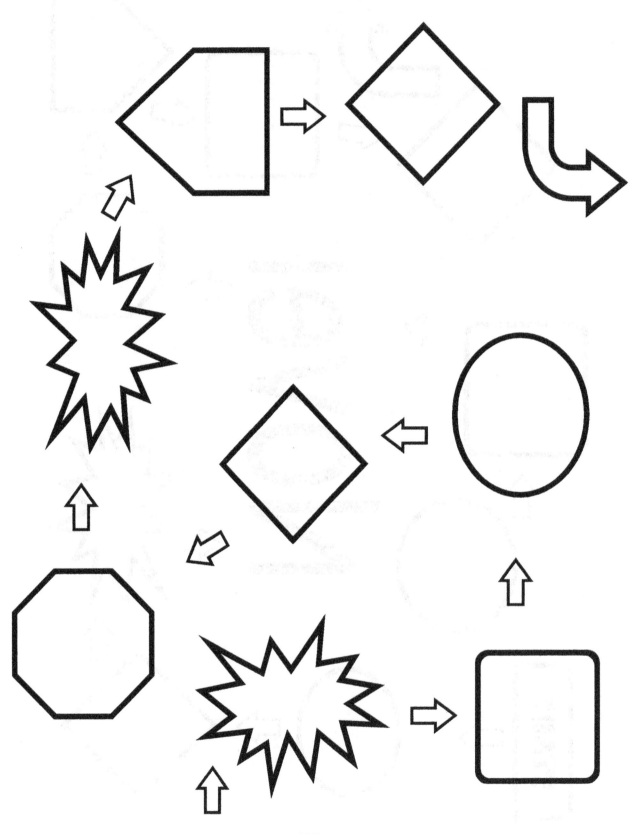

72

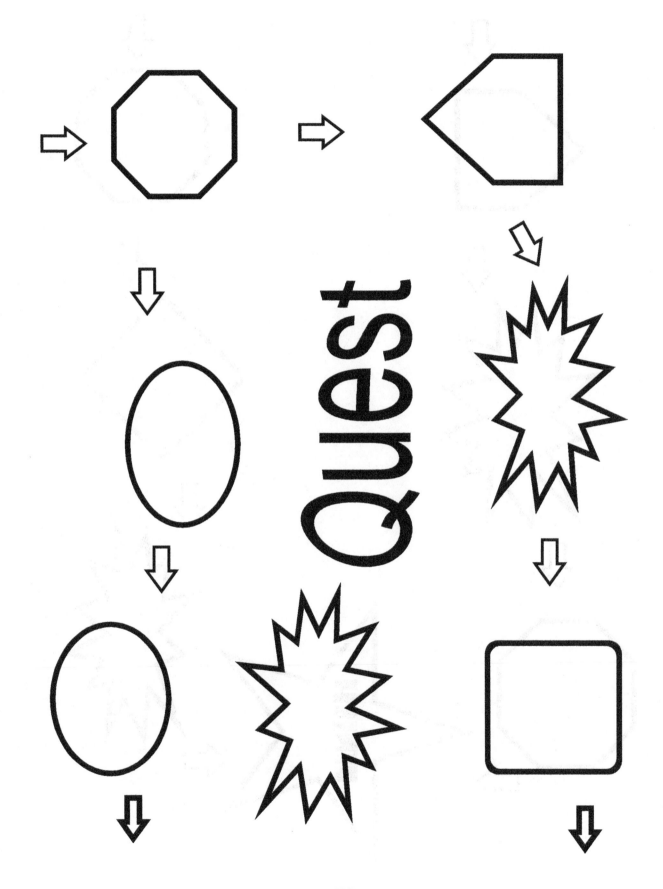

Quest

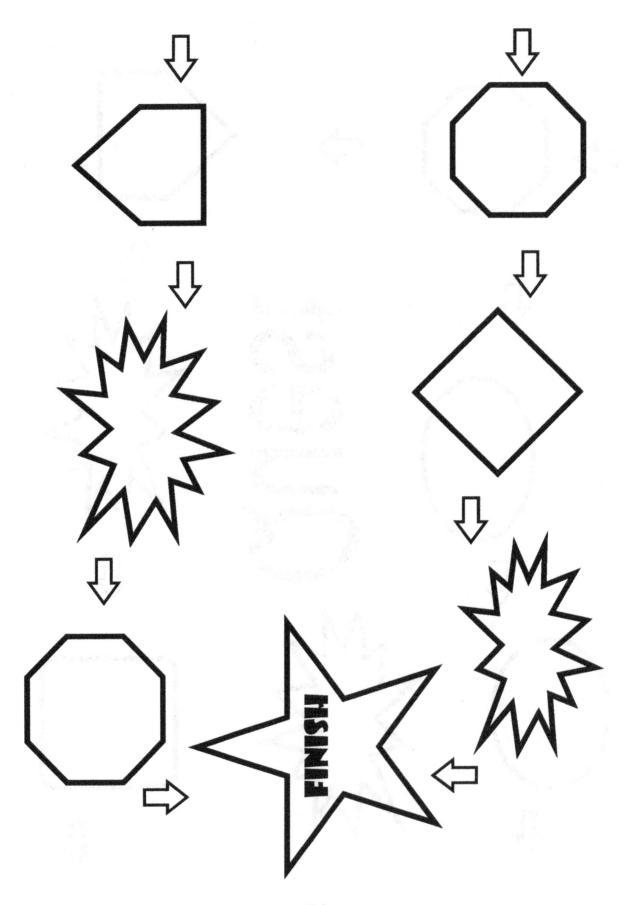

FINISH

How would using a different point of view to tell the story have changed this book?

Share your thoughts about the vocabulary contained in this novel. How did it contribute to the overall quality of the story?

Describe the point of view from which the story was told. Why do you think the author chose to write the book in that way?

Go around the group and share what you'd like to ask this author about his or her work.

Have a race and find an example of a simile or metaphor used by the author. Share aloud.

How did this author create believable characters?

Publishers get thousands of manuscripts a year. Give 3 reasons why you think they chose to publish this book.

Share a few lines in the novel you think are especially well-written. Explain your choice.

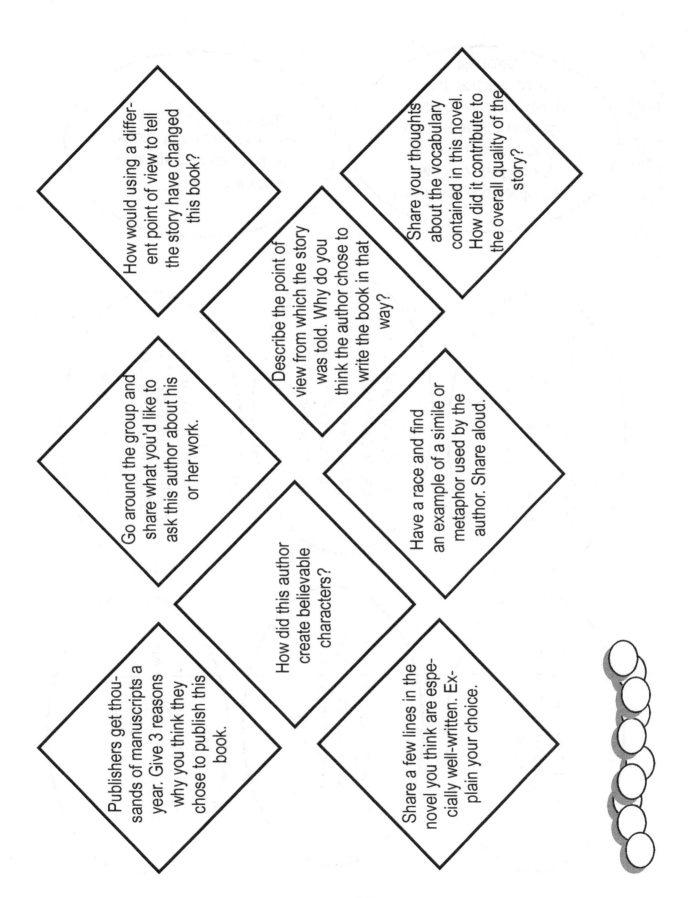

75

Did the author use any symbols or objects to help communicate the theme? Describe.

What might you guess about the author's personal beliefs as a result of reading this story?

What is the major theme or message communicated in the story?

Take 60 seconds and brainstorm with the group about other novels you've read that have a strong central message or theme.

How do you feel about the idea or theme in the story? Do you have any personal experiences that have shaped your view on this?

Why do you think the author chose this title? Have each player give the novel a new title. Discuss their meanings.

Select 5 powerful words to describe the ideas shared through this book. Have one other player do the same.

Tolerance and freedom are two important literary themes. Together, brainstorm at least 5 more BIG ideas or lessons used as common themes in literature.

Will this book still be popular in 30 years? Why or why not?

What criteria do the members of your group have for a good book? Using those guidelines, how does each player rate this book?

Describe two things the author did to maintain your interest in the book.

Go around the group and have each player respond to this prompt: This book made me believe that...

What lesson did you learn from the characters that would help you in your own life? Pick one other player to answer this same question.

What do you think prompted the author to write a book such as this one?

Do you think a book needs a clear theme in order to be powerful or memorable? Explain your thinking and give examples to support your opinion.

77

Copyright 2003 Pieces of Learning

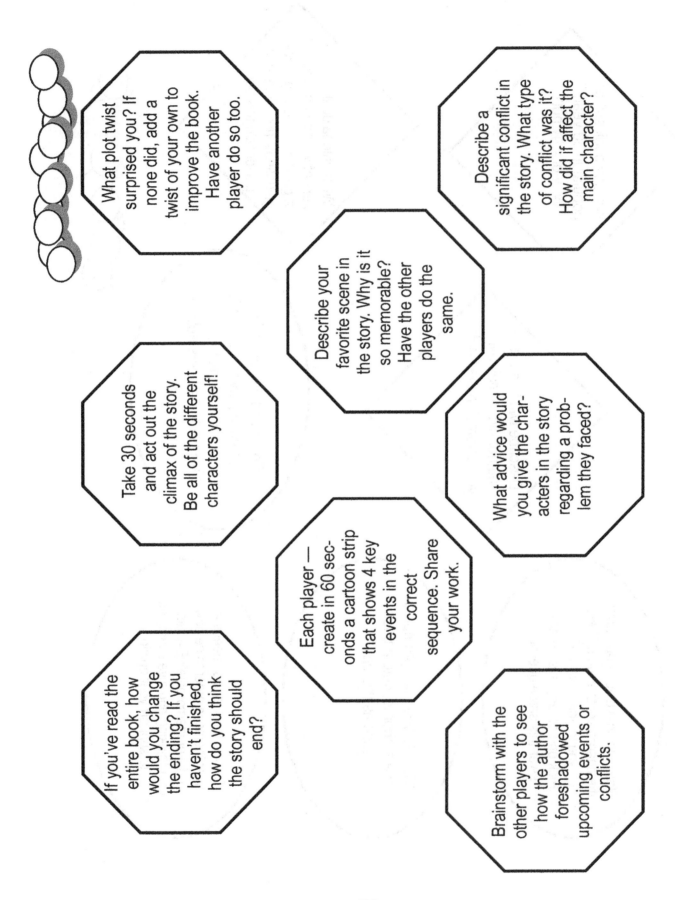

What plot twist surprised you? If none did, add a twist of your own to improve the book. Have another player do so too.

Describe a significant conflict in the story. What type of conflict was it? How did if affect the main character?

Describe your favorite scene in the story. Why is it so memorable? Have the other players do the same.

Take 30 seconds and act out the climax of the story. Be all of the different characters yourself!

What advice would you give the char-acters in the story regarding a prob-lem they faced?

Each player — create in 60 sec-onds a cartoon strip that shows 4 key events in the correct sequence. Share your work.

If you've read the entire book, how would you change the ending? If you haven't finished, how do you think the story should end?

Brainstorm with the other players to see how the author foreshadowed upcoming events or conflicts.

78

Take 60 seconds to create a group web about a minor character. Pass the paper around to add ideas.

All players—tell what you think the main character's favorite song would be and why.

Explain which two characters in the story are the most different and why.

Take 60 seconds and sketch a character in the story. Include 3 symbolic items in it that tell about him/her.

Create an invisible character bag for someone in the story. What 5 items would you include in it and why?

In what way does a character in the story remind you of someone you know?

Create 3 questions you could ask the author that would help you better understand one of the main characters.

Who is your favorite character and why? Tell about him/her in a 30 second commercial.

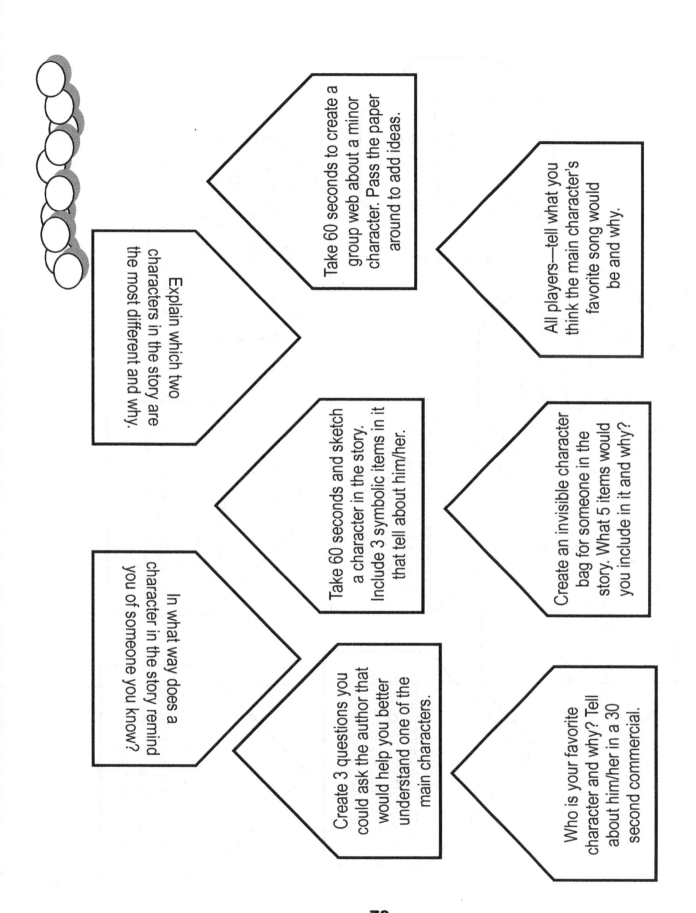

79

Develop three quality questions about the plot you feel any reader should be able to answer. Ask the other players to respond to them.

Be the main character. Answer one question from each player. Their questions should focus on how you as the main character think and feel about the events, problems and other characters in the book.

Imagine this book as a movie. Which 3 scenes from the story would make excellent previews and why?

All players—describe what you would give each of the main characters as a birthday gift and why.

Predict what the main characters will be doing 10 years after the story concludes. Choose another player to answer this too.

Summarize the entire story in 30 seconds!

Name three things that are very important to each of the main characters in the story. Explain your choices.

If you were in the main character's position at the climax of the story, what would you have done?

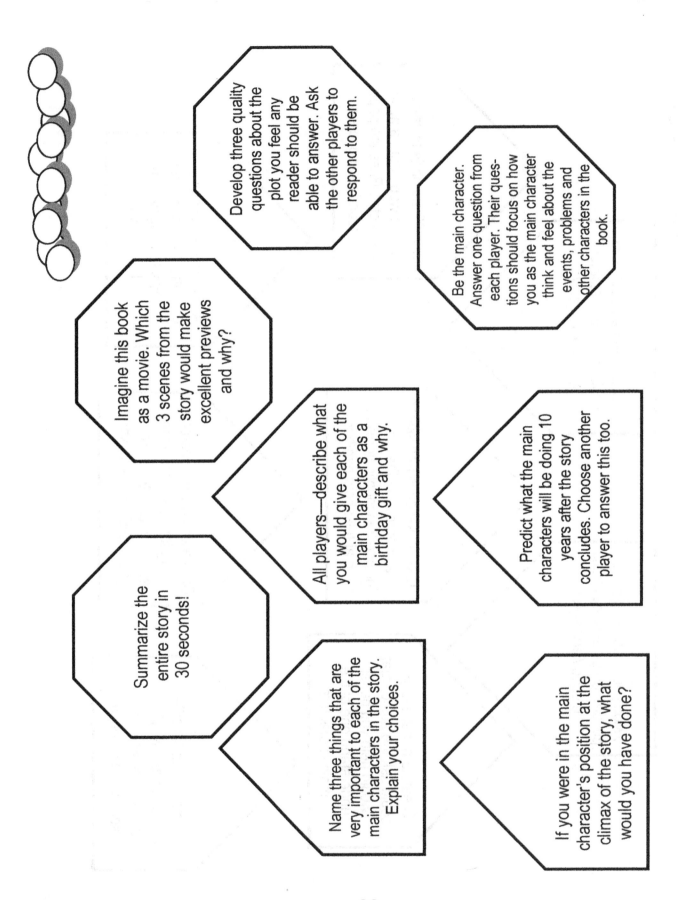

80

Everyone take 60 seconds and create a quick sketch or map that provides key information about the setting of the story. Share.

What time of year and in what time period is your novel set? What clues did the author give that helped you determine this?

How would you describe the overall mood of the novel? What did the author do to create this mood?

How would changing the place or time in which the story takes place affect the plot?

Find a passage to share that does an excellent job of describing the setting of the novel.

Tell the group about a novel you've read that had an especially interesting setting. How much impact did the time and/or place have on the novel you're discussing today?

What clues does the author provide about the cultural or social background of the characters in the story?

Go around the group 3 times and have each player give a precise adjective that describes the setting of the story.

If you could change one thing about the setting of the novel what would it be? Have the other players explain how your choice would affect the story.

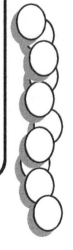

81

Using only motions, portray the key character dealing with an important conflict in the story. Let the others guess what you're communicating.

Create a short poem or commercial message in which you correctly use at least 3 new vocabulary words.

In 60 seconds, pose 4 comprehension questions and have other players answer them.

Work with a partner and write lyrics relating to the story that fit the tune of "Mary had a Little Lamb" or "Row Row Row Your Boat". Perform it for each other.

All players—grade this book on 4 things: characterization, plot, interest level, and writer's skill.

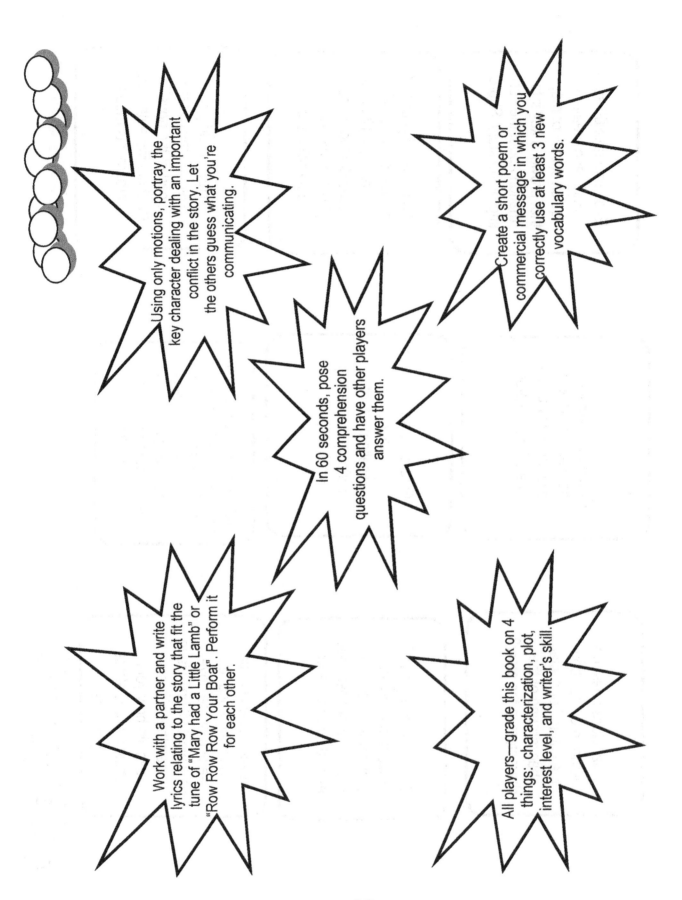

82

Tell 2 ways in which you're like and 2 ways in which you're different from one of the characters in the novel. Now choose another player to do the same.

Perform a 30 second commercial in which you encourage people to either read, or avoid reading, this book.

Pretend you have personally joined the cast of characters in the book. Describe how you fit in the story and how your presence affects the action.

Choose two of the vocabulary words learned through this book. Use them in a brief conversation with another player.

83

Go around the group and have each player comment on how a conflict in this story compares to a real life experience or challenge they've had.

Describe the problems or conflicts that occurred in the story as a direct result of the setting.

How would your family feel about living in the time and place where the story was set?

All players— take turns and walk for 15 seconds near your table in the way you feel a key character from the book would move. (Proudly, timidly, etc.)

In 30 seconds, list as many adjectives as you can to describe a character in the book. Challenge one other player to beat your score

84

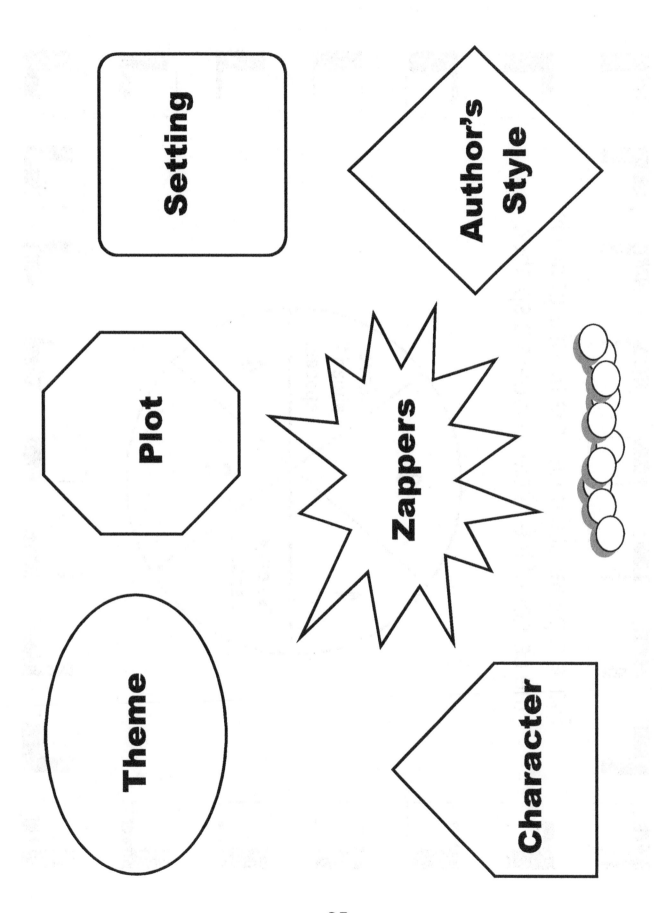

Setting

Author's Style

Plot

Zappers

Theme

Character

Place a paper clip under the tip of a pencil in the center of the circle to create a spinner.

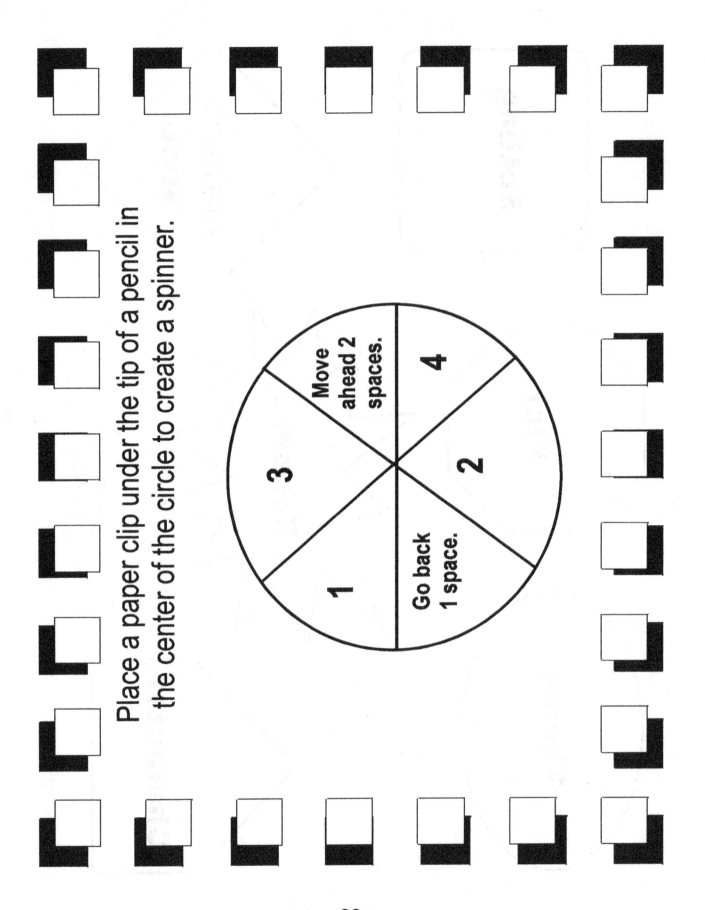